C   FOR   LEGE

CONFUSION

KING

CARING FOR

CONFUSION

Paulette Micklewood BA, BSc

Based on the experience of caring for her mother

Illustrated by Kaye Watson

Scutari Press · London

© Scutari Press 1991

A division of Scutari Projects, the publishing company of the Royal College of
Nursing

First published 1991

British Library Cataloguing in Publication Data
Micklewood, Paulette
 Caring for confusion.
 1. Alzheimer's disease victims. Care – Biographies
 I. Title
 362.1968983092

 ISBN 1-871364-43-4

Typeset by Photo-graphics, Honiton, Devon
Printed in Great Britain by St Edmundsbury Press Ltd
Bury St Edmunds, Suffolk

CONTENTS

Dedication

To my mother, Fay Lang Micklewood,
and to my many friends who made
caring possible through their help,
particularly Ruth Strong and the stud-
ents from Oxford Colleges, inspired
by Denis Hilton of St Anne's College.

Foreword

I had hoped to write an Introduction to this book, but recent health problems have prevented this. However, the subject is an important one that interests me, so instead I am writing this short introductory letter to say I feel sure that the hints on how Paulette coped with caring for her mother, with Kaye's evocative illustrations, will help those who are still caring for someone.

When I meet afflicted people I meet my own inadequacy. The gap between what I am and what I ought to be is clear and painful. I try to do the right thing. I think about them and how I can help them or be of service. I feel I ought to cheer them up, though with what I do not know, for I have no great resources of cheer within me. So sometimes I become hearty instead and apply more ointment to my ego than thought to their problems. I can't tell you, therefore, how I have helped them, because I haven't. I can only tell you of how they have helped me. It is right to think about such things, for who knows when affliction no longer means them or us but me?

From afflicted people I learned a very valuable lesson, about which there is a conspiracy of silence. Many problems just have no answer, so it's no use trying to invent one. You can only learn to live with the problems or transcend them. It's no use saying they will go away and that there is a happy ending in this world for everyone – for this is not true – though you can try for it. If you are visiting an afflicted person, over-hopeful chatter gets you off the hook, if your visit isn't too long, but you can tell by the expression on people's faces that they know you're playing the game to help yourself, not to help them.

I send my best wishes to all those loving people who are caring for sufferers of this dreadful disease.

Rabbi Lionel Blue

Adapted from *Bright Blue* by Rabbi Lionel Blue with the permission of BBC Enterprises.

MY MOTHER

Like an old-fashioned film
Scenes flicker past but make no sense.
Nothing follows on as it should,
People change like actors in a play
First they seem to be one – then another.
What is the time? the year? the day?
All is a maze – but does it matter?
I hold life's candle and watch it gutter
Burning – oh so slowly.
Soon there will be a welcome release
Filled with eternal peace.

By Paulette Micklewood

GENERAL INTRODUCTION

This booklet describes how I cared for my mother when she had Alzheimer's disease and has come from practical experience. The information may be helpful to people who are caring for individuals with similar conditions or problems.

As Alzheimer's disease causes degeneration of the nerve cells in the brain, it affects many vital functions, including memory, emotions and the control of physical functions. Its progress is long, slow and relentless. At the moment there is no known cure. It is one of the major causes of dementia, whether pre-senile or senile, and in rare cases can occur in someone as young as 22 years old. Dementia is not a normal part of ageing; anyone who has it is ill and needs to be assessed by a specialist as it can have many causes. These include things as simple as vitamin deficiency, which may be curable. The Alzheimer's Disease Society (address in Part 3) has a research fund to which contributions can be made; it must be specified if the money is only to go to medical research.

Alzheimer's disease is a very distressing condition for families who have to face the continuing 24-hour task of caring. They may not always understand the problems of the relative for whom they are caring, and sometimes view his or her behaviour as deliberate rather than as the consequence of illness. Also, many of the medical and paramedical profession view the carer as over-protective or motivated by feelings of guilt, and they seem to overlook the fact that the carer may be motivated by LOVE for the individual for whom they are caring.

Some or all of the following difficulties may be encountered by sufferers: anxiety, disorientation, memory problems, bizarre behaviour, emotional disturbance, social withdrawal and self-neglect, aggressiveness and beligerence and speech loss.

Although I was caring for a woman, only a few of the remarks are not equally relevant to caring for a man. In the early stages there is only a little dementia with longer stretches of lucidity, but as the disease progresses it is noticeable that behaviour changes from day to day. In my mother's case she was very practical in her attitude; she was aware 'there was something wrong with her head' so when she did something strange I reminded her that 'your head is bothering you again'. She never showed fear, which some sufferers do. Reactions are bound to be different from one person to another as the different parts of the brain seem to be affected in a random order, although the picture is the same at the end, sufferers being unable to name their own family and being doubly incontinent. My mother never lost her ability to speak, so most of the damage to her brain must have been on the right-hand side, whereas some people have more damage to the left-hand side and lose their speech early in the illness. The amygdala, which controls aggression, was adversely affected in my mother for only six months, but aggressive behaviour can last for years in some cases. Every sufferer has to be looked at and responded to individually as their needs and problems are, to a certain extent, unique.

My mother was often aware in the early stages of her illness that she was becoming confused, and one day she suddenly said to me that I could write anything I liked about her after she had gone, if it would help others; she insisted that I took notes. At the time I did not think that I would use them, but she was right. I have written this book and I hope that it will help other carers.

Looking back, I realise, the first thing I noticed that was unusual was that she planted a rose upside down. She was a keen gardener, and I tried to convince myself that this was all right as it was autumn and both ends

Figure 1

of the rose looked similar and I had to look very closely to see why it looked peculiar. However, I could not overlook the fact that the roots were thinner and had no thorns. First signs may vary from one person to another.

The next things that were not 'right' were complaints that her head hurt and dreams that seemed real to her. She also thought that some items in the house (a big plant and two refrigerators) were having a powerful influence over her and started compiling shopping lists, which involved lots of little notes: there could be 30 scraps of paper on the kitchen work-top and half of these would say 'Bread'. My mother then became convinced that her close friend next door had taken such things as her engagement ring and a worn-out bath mat. This then developed into general anxiety about the thought that there were intruders downstairs and that she had no money to buy food. She started hiding what money she had around the house, as well as hiding her keys. Her general behaviour became unreliable and she started to do things such as going in next door while still wearing her dressing gown. Three electric kettles were burnt dry as my mother had forgotten to put water in them.

I cared continuously for my mother during the last seven years of her

Figure 2

life, and for much of that time she did not know who I was, although she always knew I was familiar; sometimes, she thought I was her sister, which was unfortunate as they used to fight as children and this reinforced the unco-operative side of her behaviour.

For years, my mother would ask me, 'Where is Paulette?' or say that she had never been married and, at other times, that she had never had any children. Every time, I reminded her gently of the truth and gave her a cuddle and a smile as she needed to be reassured on these occasions.

As I desperately needed the support of friends we moved from Devon to Oxford, which resulted in a year's complete confusion for my mother. During this period, she thought that her mother was living with us, which created new problems. On occasions, for example, if I prepared a meal, we could not start eating because her mother had not come, or she would complain that I had not laid a place for her mother. At other times she would not go out as her mother was not ready, or else she was wanting to rush out as her mother had already left. I found that diversion was the only answer to this sort of problem and would give her something else to do or look at; as a rule, this quickly obliterated her previous thoughts and she forgot her mother or whatever else was bothering her, for a short while anyway. In Devon, however, it was 'her' house and everything had to be done as she said, even when wrong, so at least the move to Oxford removed one of our problems.

Another major problem for my mother could have been one of role reversal, as I was now caring for her when previously it was she who had cared for me. In solving this, I found that what I had learnt in my psychology degree came in useful. Instead of calling her 'Mummy', which always came out sounding cross as she was no longer fulfilling this role, I called her 'dear' or some other familiar form of endearment. Also, I thought myself positively into the role of 'carer' and not 'daughter'. The role I had assumed rarely slipped and it made caring so much easier as I did not have the emotional conflicts that so many people find absolutely draining. Another psychological trick was that I always thought of it as *her* illness and did not take responsibility for it; although I was helping her, the illness remained her problem.

If I wanted to go out, I would find someone else to come in to care for my mother, but I never told her this. Instead, I would say, 'So-and-so is coming to tea this afternoon, and I am going out, so will you look after her please?' This always worked well and, although she often forgot where I was and who visitors were, it was never too difficult for them to remind her that I would be back soon and that she was entertaining them to tea. My mother was never aggressive with visitors, and it is worth remembering that most sufferers save such behaviour for those they know and are on their 'best behaviour' with strangers. I never left my mother with anyone until they had been to tea with us and were familiar to her and knew our routines.

If the sufferer has to attend a medical appointment and transport is required, it is important when booking the hospital car or ambulance to ensure that an additional seat is booked for the carer or whoever will be acting as escort. At times, there can be a lack of understanding shown by the driver who may make upsetting remarks such as, 'Coming along for the ride, then?' or, 'How nice to be coming too', when in fact one would rather be getting on with one's own affairs.

The importance of having an escort was reinforced when my mother, on several occasions, sounded most convincing when she wanted to be set down at the wrong place. If I had not been with her, it could easily have happened and she would have been completely lost in a strange part of the city, claiming to 'visit' a non-existent friend. My mother looked perfectly well for years before her illness became apparent. However, she suffered memory loss and was unable to tell anyone about her recent symptoms, what medication she was taking or events in her life, so it was essential that she had an escort whenever she left the house.

As we had moved house, I was not prepared to disorientate my mother further by organising respite care while I took a holiday. I realised that this would result in an increase in her confusion with which I would have to cope later, and taking her with me would have been no holiday. However, individuals' circumstances are quite different and, for some, the break is worthwhile and compensates for the increased confusion that may result for a while when the sufferer first returns home. Reminiscence therapy may in the same way add to confusion (see p. 41) for some people.

My advice to carers is to take each minute as it comes and to cope with that. Do not waste energy worrying about the next day or the future but think about your own interests as you care. It is important to retain or develop your own interests and hobbies so that personal identity is kept and you are not swamped by caring. Hobbies can include anything from gardening or stamp collecting to reading, as these would be equally effective as a diversion from caring, providing that the carer perseveres. Who knows, you might even become an expert on that subject. I chose to do courses with the Open University and I can still remember a health visitor's surprise when, in response to something she said, I replied, 'Good gracious, I don't have to think about it all the time; I fill my mind with something that challenges it'.

While pursuing your interest or hobby, it is essential if possible to have someone in to give you a break for your chosen occupation, even if you do not need to leave the house. Age Concern can usually refer you to an individual or agency who can help, even if they cannot be of assistance themselves (see Part 3).

When something goes right or is enjoyed by the sufferer, however small this may be, it should be acknowledged as a major achievement by the carer. 'Job satisfaction' helps, even when it is based on a few fleeting moments of success; in fact, this makes those occasions even more precious.

A sense of humour is vital and should be cultivated, as it helps to see the absurd side. There were many times when I needed mine, such as when

I opened the door to a taxi driver to find, on returning upstairs to fetch my mother, that she had put lipstick around her eyes instead of on her lips. On another occasion when I turned my back for a second, she took off all her clothes after I had just spent half an hour getting her dressed. In both cases, after my first horrified cry, I just giggled, gave her a cuddle and started to deal with the situation as quicky as possible.

Even with a sense of humour, it is possible for carers to be reduced to tears. I tended to shed a tear on occasions when I was moved, as I did two days before my mother died when I gave her a primrose plant to look at and smell and she spoke her last word, saying, 'Lovely'.

Love, patience, fortitude and stamina are also very necessary to a carer. It is easy to feel resentment at the responses of an individual with Alzheimer's disease, and some carers do feel like this. However, although this is understandable, it rarely helps anyone and often only creates antagonism. Rather like someone who shouts at another person or becomes aggressive but elicits little or no response which provokes anger, so, too, will the carer simply become more frustrated at the absence of an appropriate reaction.

My mother was aggressive for six months, but I always understood that she was not really trying to break my arm, for instance, but that the part of her brain controlling aggression was being affected. She was never aggressive with anyone except me, and always when we were on our own, so it was no problem when people visited. Ruth Bennett of Columbia University was right when she told a conference that 'care giving is not for the faint at heart or the frail of body'.

Some people feel anger that they have been singled out to care, which does not help the situation and can be counter-productive. In my case, I did not feel like this as I had no dependants and could enjoy feeling that it was a chance for me to return some of the love and care that my mother had given me when I was a tiny, helpless baby. This may not have been possible had I been caring for a family of my own. My mother's gift to me was to make me a much more caring and compassionate person.

The sufferer's loss of social graces can embarrass others and, for this reason, it is often difficult to entertain or go out visiting friends. One example I always remember is my mother being asked to a birthday tea, where there was a lovely lace tablecloth on the table, and tea included raspberries and cream. The tablecloth was not quite its spotless self by the time she finished. However, as long as one has warned friends in advance about the situation, there is little more that one can do.

The carer has to be vigilant when shopping and keep a careful eye on the individual to ensure that nothing is inadvertently taken, as cash is often a forgotten commodity. This happened to me more than once when I was out with my mother. On one occasion, at the cash desk where I was doing my usual quick check, I found a packet of biscuits in my mother's quite small handbag; yet I had not seen her take them, nor would I have thought they could have fitted into the bag. A way to overcome this problem is to go mostly to shops where the situation can be explained. I found that my local shops could not have been more helpful. Also, as a precaution, I carried a letter from our GP, which explained my mother's medical problem, but I never had to show this to a shopkeeper as my mother's condition was so obvious.

At a later stage in my mother's illness, when she could no longer walk to the shops, but was not immobile, I would rush out to the local shops for essentials while she was still asleep and return as quickly as possible before she woke. The local shopkeepers were very helpful and always let me go the head of the queue, and a friend did the rest of my shopping in the town centre once a week.

When caring for someone with Alzheimer's disease, one is bound to feel sadness over a relationship that has changed so drastically, but there is no need to feel guilt for losing patience or for sometimes getting angry. It is inevitable that carers will experience these emotions at times, especially when tired. Sometimes they feel guilty because they think they have not done absolutely everything that could be done for the sufferer. It is important to remember that no-one could cater for every need of the individual and, usually, the carer is doing more than could be expected anyway. At times like this, I just reminded myself that I was human too, and therefore fallible, and I did the best I could for my mother under the circumstances.

Repetition is usually one of the most frustrating things for carers of individuals suffering from Alzheimer's disease. It is impossible for sufferers to stop repeatedly asking the same question. My solution to this problem was to reply to my mother once or twice and then to produce a diversion that would distract her attention. This diversionary tactic could be to encourage her to watch television, look at a picture in a magazine or newspaper, admire a flower in the garden or listen to music, which is a great soother. These techniques never failed to work, and if it was an object that was causing the problem, I moved it to where it could not be seen for the time being. It is as well to remember that it must be much worse to feel so disorientated and to be caught in such a 'groove', even if the sufferer is not fully aware of it.

Mealtimes can create problems, and it is important to remember only to serve the food that you actually want eaten; if Alzheimer's disease sufferers see a whole loaf or bowl full of sugar, some are liable to eat it all. In my case, I did not have this particular problem but the reverse, as my mother had to be tempted to eat anything; perhaps this was a reversion to childhood when she had been difficult to feed. She started to do things she had done as a child such as hiding food or, forgetting that I had cooked the meal, asking for my help in discarding it. She would say, for instance, 'Where is Dick?' (a Great Dane she had as a child who obviously used to help her out) or, 'Quickly, is there a flower vase I can put this in?'; these occasions should be treated with humour and patience.

However, it is important to ensure that you both eat well and that you have a varied, well-balanced diet containing food such as wholemeal pastas, wholemeal bread, pulses, unrefined sugar, brown rice, fruit and vegetables. These should be eaten in preference to such foods as white bread, fats, white sugar and salt, which should only be eaten in small quantities. A balanced diet will help the carer to retain the high energy levels necessary for looking after the individual and it will also help normal bodily functions and reduce the risk of certain illnesses. Avoiding constipation by means of a high-fibre diet will help to lessen the confusion that can be experienced by any elderly person with sluggish bowel function.

Practical and physical aspects of caring for a person suffering from Alzheimer's disease, such as how to mark the edge of stairs safely and how to keep hair clean when washing it is no longer tolerated, will be covered in Part 2 of this book. However, it is essential that the emotional needs of the sufferer are not disregarded and that the carer caters for these as well. My mother, for example, loved toys, but, as I knew from my study of psychology an elderly person should not be treated as a child but as an adult, I would not readily have bought her a toy. I suspect that I, along with many others, felt like this in order to protect myself from the knowledge that, if ill with Alzheimer's disease, we may revert to childish ways. I later modified my views when, shortly after I had come home to care for my mother, I attended a cancer research fund-raising coffee morning, where I bought a large pink elephant with one of my friends' children in mind. When I brought it home, my mother just stood and looked at it; then she said, 'Oh...' and put out a hand to stroke it. In that moment I realised that my mother wanted the toy, and I suddenly knew where the elephant was going. I asked my mother if she would like it and she said, 'Yes please' with great enthusiasm, and called her Pinky.

At first Pinky stood on top of my mother's wardrobe, but it was not long before she was taken to bed by my mother, where she was a very useful prop for her head, and this is where she stayed until the end of my mother's life. Pinky gave emotional security as she was always there, which I could not be, and she became a 'friend' or mother-substitute. The great advantages that Pinky had over the pet recommended by the experts were that she was always there, she could not be hurt when pulled along and she could not scratch or bite. My cat, Fluffy, was never accepted by my mother. She always stroked Fluffy the wrong way, something she did not do with any other cat, so it was clearly a display of jealousy. Fortunately, Fluffy did not like my mother either so they both avoided each other.

As Pinky was such a great success, other toys were added to my mother's collection over the years, different types fulfilling different needs. More recently, I have read an article in the Canadian Alzheimer's Disease Society's newsletter recommending toys, and I am sure that this is right, provided that the sufferer wants them, as they can fill a real need.

In psychology one is taught that everybody needs a certain amount of 'personal space', but this is something one lacks as the carer of an Alzheimer's disease sufferer, as they will follow you around, like a shadow, most of the time. This can present many problems for the carer, but it is no good if he or she becomes anxious or tense about it. The best thing to do is to try to relax and to give the sufferer a cuddle as this is the natural thing to do when anyone is so very close. Also, it is important to remember that this type of behaviour is usually a cry for reassurance. However, it is also important for carers to ensure that someone takes over from them occasionally, so that they can have breaks outside the house where they can have some 'personal space'.

Some experts advise labelling objects and writing notes (Reality Orientation) to help the sufferer, but this is of very limited use in Alzheimer's disease. Although it will work for a while in the very early stages, it can be a cause of real frustration for the carer when the sufferer does not live up to expectations. I used to leave a large note in capital letters on my mother's lap saying, 'I have gone to the shops; back in ten minutes', but the note was very soon always to be found on the floor, sometimes crumpled up. My mother would deny having seen it, although I knew we had read it together before I went out. Sometimes, she would not seem to have noticed my short absence, but at other times she would say, 'Oh there you are, I have been wondering where you were' and would sound quite upset. I realised as a result of this that, in future, she must always go out with me or have someone to stay with her while I was out of the house.

When I went out with my mother, I always took extreme care not to lose her, but, despite this caution, it did happen twice when I visited the ladies toilets. On the first occasion, I found that my mother had gone, and I ran out of the shop to see her about 200 yards away, walking quickly up the street. The second time it happened, I found her in another department of a big store urging everyone to look for *me*. After that, I decided that I must keep her with me by retaining her interest so, whenever I visited the toilet, I talked to her continuously through the door. Later, it became necessary to take her in with me. This would have been more of a problem had she been a man, when I would have needed help from another man.

Sometimes my mother would talk about her own mother as if she were still alive. When this happened, I tried to bring my mother back to reality by saying that her mother had gone to Heaven, and, as this was a concept she knew from childhood, the strategy usually worked. However, attempting to 'shape' her behaviour in this way (behavioural training) only worked in a limited way and for a short while in the early stages.

A few people feel they have to 'keep up appearances', but this cannot be sustained over a long period as it would be an intolerable strain on the carer. There is no need for the carer to feel embarrassed by the sufferer's behaviour. The carer should explain to people that dementia is an illness affecting the brain and is not an inevitable consequence of old age. 'Fair-weather' friends will drift away, but those that remain loyal are pure gold and these are the ones worth cherishing.

Some people find caring lonely. Overcoming loneliness is a very personal matter but it can help to involve other people in your life. Some rely on friendship whereas others develop other means of overcoming the problem.

I drew inner strength and overcame loneliness by my belief in God. I never felt lonely because I always felt I had an unseen protector to whom I could turn. If I was unable to move my mother, I always asked God to help. It always seemed to work for me; I cannot say she became lighter, or unseen hands helped – it might just have been an increase in the flow of adrenaline.

Often carers doubt their ability to cope; professionals rarely reassure them by saying that they are giving the best care possible, which is usually the truth as professionals cannot give care on a one-to-one basis. I worried that I might be depriving my mother of professional care and would have been relieved to know that *loving* care is the best that can be given. Joining the Alzheimer's Disease Society can help as current problems can be discussed with people who have already been through similar difficulties. Problems and reactions vary, depending on the degree of brain damage, and some sufferers can demonstrate fear, which, fortunately, my mother did not seem to experience. It is impossible to have an accurate knowledge of how a sufferer feels and much must be based on observation of that person. This is where you may find it helpful to discuss with other people their solutions in a similar situation. It does not matter if you are unable to attend meetings, as it is possible to telephone your local contact, and in some places any member of the local committee, to ask them for advice. If one member has not met a specific problem, there is almost certainly someone else who has.

Alzheimer's disease is a dreadful illness for anyone to have, and watching someone you love struggling with it can never be easy. However, as I have said before, carers should not feel guilty if they sometimes become irritable or 'snappy', as this is usually the result of over-tiredness and is quite understandable. It is important for carers to cater for their own needs as well, by finding someone who will replace them for a short while so that they can have a break away from it all and replenish themselves emotionally and physically. It is important to keep fit; I found Sanatogen (the original powder) a great help as a tonic, but everyone will have a favourite remedy for tiredness. If you have any aches try relaxing those muscles; massage from a trained person should help. You need to keep fit for both your sakes.

When the patient eventually dies it is natural for many carers to feel relieved as it is doubtful that there was any pleasure left in the sufferer's life and the person they were had been lost long before. In the last few weeks they were probably very ill, and carers should not feel guilty about their sense of relief – this is compassion. Towards the end of her life, my mother could not even manage to watch the television at the end of her bed that had given her so much enjoyment, and I could not have wished her to struggle on any further. Like many others, my grief and mourning was experienced earlier in my mother's illness when, most of the time, she still resembled the person she had been before developing the disease.

There are many caring organisations that can give helpful advice, and these are listed in Part 3 of this book. One of the major ones is the Alzheimer's Disease Society, and, even if you are not able to attend local meetings, it is important to join the Society as it provides a national monthly newsletter, which has hints and addresses that may be helpful.

Part 2 of this book is divided into sections covering the early, middle and late stages of the disease. The purpose behind this is that carers can choose to ignore the later sections should they find it upsetting to read about the future course of the disease. Alternatively, they may wish to know the answers to the problems I encountered, and these are covered in the appropriate sections. I hope these will be useful to carers.

Remember that, even when sufferers are unable to do or understand anything, as a nurse said, 'They are still capable of being loved'.

PRACTICAL HINTS FOR CARERS

The Early Stages

The early stages can be, for the carer, the most difficult stages in Alzheimer's disease, as the affected individual looks completely normal and any erratic behaviour may be consistent with normal old age. A friend or relative who sees only one or two changes can be fooled into thinking that it is the carer who is 'peculiar' and not the sufferer. (However, this will not be the case with a younger sufferer as behavioural changes would not then be expected so the problem is apparent earlier.) It is the overall clinical picture, covering all areas of the individual's problems and behaviour, that alerts the geriatric or psychiatric specialist to the possibility of Alzheimer's disease. It is important that a specialist should see the sufferer as other causes of dementia can be identified and often treated.

Problems experienced by the individual may include:

- memory loss

- confusion

- aggression

- threatening to commit suicide

- loss of balance

- meaningless shouting

- laughing or crying inappropriately

- wandering off

- groping at things with the hands

- loss of ability to handle money

- losing money

- inability to do simple familiar tasks such as dressing and undressing.

Many different problems may affect the individual and these will vary between people. The stages at which they manifest themselves also vary, and some may not appear at all; it depends on which parts of the brain are affected and at which stage in the illness. As the brain controls both emotional and physical activities, the sufferer will have problems covering the whole spectrum of these, and will have to cope with areas as diverse as aggression and incontinence.

It is impossible to tell how the sufferer feels, but, from observation, it seems to vary between people, particularly in the early stages when there is still more lucidity than dementia. My mother was aware there was something wrong with her head, and was very practical in her attitude to the problem. When something went wrong, she responded very positively when I reminded her that 'your head is bothering you again', and she accepted this explanation.

Reactions are bound to vary, though, as they depend on which parts of the brain have been affected and how badly, although the picture at the end is approximately the same for all. For example, my mother never lost the power of speech and was, therefore, probably not badly affected in the left hemisphere of her brain, part of which controls speech; others lose their speech early. However, what she said had often lost its meaning to her; for example she would shout the Lord's Prayer repeatedly whereas others may repeat childhood rhymes. Also the amygdala, which controls aggression, was adversely affected in my mother for only six months, but in others aggressive behaviour has been known to last for years. Every sufferer has to be looked at and regarded as an individual as his or her needs and problems are unique.

As the memory fails, the sufferer may feel panic-stricken and seize the carer's wrist or forearm, which can be very painful. To release the grip, the carer should lift his or her arm up as high as possible and bring it down fast. This causes pressure against the patient's thumb and causes him to let go. Caution must be exercised so that the grip release is not carried out in an angry or aggressive manner because violent movement can be harmful to the frail patient and can hurt. Reassurance can be given by touch or by a hug when this is appropriate.

Do not expect the patient with Alzheimer's disease to know who you are. Even a son or husband can be thought to be someone else, and difficult behaviour may be directed against that person and not at you, the carer. If asked, 'Do you know who I am?', the answer is nearly always 'Yes', but if asked for a name or a relationship, or whether one is a friend or a relation, the reply is usually evasive. It is not unusual for the sufferer to deny ever having had children, and even to say that he or she never married; my mother used to say all of these things.

Carers need a great deal of patience. It is no good telling the patient to 'snap out of it' or to 'try harder', or to make remarks such as 'You remember' or 'You know how to do that'. In fact, the person is invariably trying so hard to achieve normality that it can be difficult at first, even for the GP, to see what is wrong as responses *seem* appropriate.

The carer who remains constantly with the sufferer will gradually notice a set pattern of 'social' responses, such as 'Thank you', 'Yes', 'No', 'Look at the rain/sun', 'I'm pleased to meet you', etc., which will appear again and again and gradually fit less and less appropriately to the current situation. It is important that the carer is aware of practical solutions to the many problems they encounter, and these are covered in the following sections.

Safety

Safety is an essential aspect of care, especially when the Alzheimer's disease sufferer becomes confused and starts to wander. At this stage, it is vital that all outer doors are kept locked so that the individual is prevented from leaving the house. It would be all too easy for that person to wander off and become lost or frightened or be robbed. Also, all door and cupboard keys should be removed and kept in a safe place, so that there is no danger of the sufferer having access to potentially dangerous things or locking himself in. Digital locks are useful as no key is needed. Clock keys should also be kept in a safe place. Bolts and keys should be removed from bathroom, lavatory or cellar doors to ensure that neither the carer nor the patient can be locked in. Simple locks for toilet seats, windows, cupboards and fridges are available from baby-care departments, and the suppliers are listed on page 44.

Some sufferers still want to drive a car, which, fortunately, was not a problem I had to face. However, for some carers, this can be a very worrying problem as the patient is invariably no longer a safe driver. There are several ways to overcome this and a garage will give advice about ways to immobilise the car. In older models, the HT lead or the rotor arm can be taken out and replaced quite easily, but this can be more difficult in modern cars. In all cases, the car keys should be removed and kept in a safe place as this will, to some extent, deter the sufferer.

Structural modifications to the house may be necessary to ensure safety when an individual develops Alzheimer's disease. Placing grab-handles and hand-rails by steps (including the back and front doorsteps) can help with both the sufferer's safety and mobility. A hand-rail should also be fixed to the inside of the stairs, and the occupational therapist may be able to supply one. Another helpful addition to the stairs is white adhesive or electrical tape, which makes the steps more clearly visible. This must be replaced as soon as it shows wear to avoid tripping.

The carer should ensure that all dangerous materials, substances or implements such as bleach, weed-killer or sharp knives are kept in locked cupboards.

It is safer to use electricity rather than gas for cooking. However, care must be taken with electric rings as latent heat can remain for a long time and make the rings very hot to touch even when they are no longer red. The risk is reduced if saucepans with cold water in them are put on top of the rings immediately after use until the rings have become cold. The

Figure 3

pans remain there so that if the electricity is switched on again they provide further protection. Kettles should be put away as these can be turned on by the sufferer and burn dry if empty.

Three-way light switches, from upstairs to downstairs, are very useful for protection, as the carer can put lights on ahead of the patient from almost any position.

Trailing wires or loose mats can be very dangerous and these should be removed or covered. However, if it is essential to keep the mats, safety netting, which can be obtained from most carpet stores, should be fixed to the back of them.

Open or electric fires are hazardous as the person with Alzheimer's disease loses any sense of danger and may, for example, stand holding a newspaper so close that it will catch fire. Fires should be protected by a large fireguard, such as the type supplied for nurseries, which can be clipped

Figure 4

securely to a ring in the wall and is not easily removed. 'Microfurnaces' (see page 43) are a good alternative, as are electric convector heaters and oil-filled radiators that can be controlled by a thermostat.

Changes to the bathroom will almost certainly be required. These could include a high lavatory seat, a frame around the lavatory, a bath-board, a bath-seat and a hand-rail, which will all aid safety (the occupational therapist will probably be able to lend these to the carer). Also, it is ideal to have a bath with handles on the sides and an adjustable wash basin that can be used when sitting or standing.

The carer should be vigilant when out of the house with the sufferer, as it can be even more difficult then to ensure personal safety. When out walking, for example, it is important to hold the sufferer's arm, even if resisted and it looks as though you are fighting, as the sufferer could easily fall and be injured.

This happened to my mother one day when we were out walking. She had no difficulty before but, unfortunately, she tripped on a paving stone and broke her arm. The problem was made worse by the fact that she did not realise that she had broken her arm and continually denied the fact.

This presented many difficulties, not least of which was that she would not keep her sling on. My solution to this was to tie the sling before I put it on her and to place a rubber sheath around the knot so that it did not rub her neck. Then I pinned the sling around my mother's elbow and added about three more safety pins, which were pushed through the sling and attached to her dress. This method of securing the sling had a number of advantages in that it immobilised my mother's arm, took up the slack in the sling and reduced the weight on her neck and collar bone. Also, I had to move the arm less as the sling was pinned around it, making it more difficult for her to slide her arm out.

In situations such as these, the district nurse, occupational therapist or GP will be able to give advice or lend equipment. However, this incident reinforced for me the importance of extra vigilance when out of the house, to ensure personal and physical safety.

Eating and drinking

People with Alzheimer's disease tend to be difficult to feed. Either they cannot remember that they have just had a meal, so immediately ask for more and easily become overweight, or they think they have just had a meal, refuse food and easily lose weight. As good nutrition is important for everyone, so it is for Alzheimer's disease sufferers. If they are well nourished, sufferers are less likely to get other illnesses, and it will also help in the prevention of problems such as pressure sores.

The poor eater can be encouraged to eat by using a very large plate so that a reasonable helping looks less. Conversely, the overweight person can be given a full, small plate that looks as though it holds more than it does.

The individual who suffers from unwanted weight gain needs constant vigilance. The fridge door should be kept locked, and food should never be left on the table or lying around elsewhere as it will be eaten. The sufferer cannot be blamed for eating the entire contents of the sugar bowl or a whole loaf if it is readily available.

An underweight person, on the other hand, requires tempting, small meals – little and often is the best way of giving food. Food that is cut up into small pieces is more likely to be eaten, and even biscuits are eaten more readily if broken into pieces ('This broken biscuit needs eating up' can be an effective encouragement). The poor eater should not be forced to eat as this will aggravate the problem. It is better to emphasise that nothing has to be finished and to tempt them with appealing foods. Jam on milk puddings and pieces of apple with meat may prove appetising. Also, foods such as pâté are nourishing and easy to eat and can be a useful source of nourishment for the poor eater. Crispbread is often enjoyed, but if this is the case, the carer should make sure that it is not put in a toaster as it will go up in flames in *seconds*. At Christmas and on other special occasions, the poor eater may be tempted by small marzipan cake decorations, instead of large petit fours, as a treat. These and other ideas can be developed in order to find tempting foods for the reluctant eater.

A liquidiser or food processor is a great help, as foods can be ground and mixed to be very fine and easily swallowed. Delicious savoury and sweet mousses can be made quickly, and, as they require less chewing, they are more likely to be eaten.

Baby cookery books can be a useful source of other ideas and may provide information for the carer of a poor eater. Also, the area health authority has a community dietician who can give advice on feeding problems for both the poor and over-enthusiastic eater, and for those with specific weight problems.

A microwave oven is very useful, as slowly consumed food and drinks, if in suitable containers, can be reheated easily. However, care must be taken that certain foods, such as chicken and red meat, are adequately defrosted if taken from the freezer. It is not advisable to reheat food more than once unless this is done in the course of one mealtime. On these occasions, the microwave oven can be used to reheat the carer's food and drinks, so numerous interruptions do not matter as much.

A larder fridge can be very useful as it does not need to be defrosted, and some modern fridges defrost automatically. A deep freeze can also be a great help as the carer can prepare food in bulk rather than being forced to cook food at each mealtime, which is very time-consuming.

The Alzheimer's disease sufferer may have difficulty in feeding as a result of early physical disability and, in such cases, the Disabled Living Foundation can give advice about equipment that is available. If the person eats slowly, a child's warmer plate (a plastic plate that is filled with hot water) can help to keep the food warm. These can be bought from most major chemists or baby-care departments, and a good one with a safe plug is sold at Boots (it makes a good hand warmer too).

Insulated picnic cups can be bought, which will keep drinks hotter for a longer period. It is also useful to have an invalid cup in the house for emergencies when the sufferer has problems with drinking, but it is important for the carer to practise using this beforehand as it is easy to swamp the patient.

Plastic table-cloths and/or large plastic place mats are always handy, and make it easy for the carer to mop up spills.

General health and hygiene

Dental care is an often neglected area of care, but it is vital that problems such as receding gums and dental caries are avoided as far as possible.

The sufferer should visit the dentist six-monthly, if this is possible, and advice should be sought about problems such as receding gums. A home visit by the dentist can be arranged if necessary (see page 37). A well-balanced diet with plenty of fresh fruit and vegetables will also aid dental care. It is important to supervise the sufferer cleaning his teeth or, if he is unable to do this himself, for the carer to take on the task (a good recommended toothpaste is Emoform). Teeth should be kept clean by brushing and flossing, and some individuals like a mouthwash as well. Dentures must also be cleaned adequately.

Medication

When medication is prescribed, it is important to inform the GP if the patient finds it difficult to swallow pills, as he will usually be able to prescribe a syrup instead. Also implements that help the person to take medication (such as those used for children) can be bought from most chemists.

Continence problems

Nearly all Alzheimer's disease sufferers become incontinent in the end, most of them doubly incontinent. Many incontinence aids can be obtained through the community nurse or health visitor, but in the early stages, there are a number of minor practical measures that can be taken. For example, when a woman starts to become incontinent, she can initially use a sanitary towel.

Some waterproof pants, which will be needed later, are plastic. They rustle a lot, cause condensation and are not very comfortable. Kanga pants, with a side Velcro opening, are best, as they are part material and part plastic and hold a pad. The side fastening is invaluable when the patient's incontinence becomes worse.

When requesting such garments, it is vital to give exact specifications, as the pants without side fastenings might be completely useless, as in the case of double incontinence (the individual with advanced dementia will often not tolerate pants being pulled up and down). Although it is possible to modify pants (for example getting a larger size, slitting the side and adding a Velcro fastening), it is preferable to get the correct ones in the first place. A commode should be placed by the bed, with a roll of soft lavatory paper.

There are various causes other than dementia which can be the problem in male incontinence. For example the doctor should check that there are no prostatic problems.

A variety of pants are available with a built-in pad which contains the urine. They are obtainable from Health Centres and the district nurses can advise you on the most suitable one to use.

Other methods which may help you are sheaths which are fitted with a drainage bag, pubic pressure flanges, or male urinals; they are available on prescription and should be fitted by specialist appliance nurses, such as those working for dispensing appliance contract centres throughout the country. If you have a problem finding one ring FREEPHONE 0800 590916 (there is no charge for this service), or for a continence advisor in the National Health Service ring the Disabled Living Foundation (see Section 3) 071–289 6111 or ask in your Health Centre.

Waste disposal

If waste is placed in plastic bags with ties, it is easier for the carer to check, before the dustmen come, that nothing precious has been thrown away by the sufferer. All waste-paper baskets should be checked before being emptied.

Pressure sores

A debilitated or relatively immobile person can develop bed sores very quickly, especially if very thin or obese. At the first sign of redness on the skin, especially on the buttocks, spine, shoulders, heels or other prominences, the carer should be alert to the possibility that it could be a bed sore developing. Although this is likely to be more of a problem during the later stages of the illness, bed sores can occur at any stage and may happen while the patient is still mobile. Emphasis should be placed on skin care, and the carer should ensure that the skin is (as far as possible) kept scrupulously clean and dry at all times, especially if the sufferer is incontinent. Sores can appear between skin folds (usually with obese people), so it is important to care for areas such as those between the buttocks and below the breasts.

Mobility is a good way of reducing the risk of sores developing. Therefore, a mobile person should be encouraged to walk around, and a chair- or bed-ridden person should be moved to a different position every two to four hours. This may be difficult or impossible for the carer to achieve, and help should be sought, if possible, for assistance or equipment to help the carer. Action is particularly urgent if the skin has split or blistered. Often it does not look like a sore when it first appears, but the redness does not go away and the carer should not delay in asking for help. The British Red Cross Society are extremely helpful and in many cases can lend carers equipment such as ripple mattresses (the large cell ones are excellent), which are very good in helping to prevent pressure sores developing.

If the skin has become red, but remains unbroken, a skin cream such as Drapolene can be used.

Bedding

If the patient becomes cold in bed, cellular wool blanket pieces can be used inside the sheets (see page 44). When incontinence becomes a problem, the bedding can be protected by IPS protective pant liner pads (these are flat oblong sheets of tissue held together by a porous cover).

Hot-water bottles are less satisfactory for general use as they become cold and can burst. If one is used, it should be covered (to protect the patient from the risk of burns) and securely fastened. When the carer is filling it, he or she should use a safety funnel which has a ring to allow the air to escape as the water goes in, thus preventing overflow (see page 44).

A length of pretty polyester/cotton over the top sheet on the bed will help to keep the sheet clean, looks attractive and is easily washed.

A triangular pillow (shaped like a boomerang) is a very good extra support in bed, and the patient can use it to lean against or when sitting on the edge of the bed. It does not slip in the way that ordinary pillows do.

Clothing

Clothing should be practical and have simple fastenings to enable the patient to dress or undress easily, or, if he or she needs help, to assist the carer in this task. During the day, a warm woollen cardigan, a woollen shawl or scarf and a rug will all help to keep the sufferer warm. Woollen cuffs or mittens keep hands warm and seal any gap at the wrists; they can be easily removed and different colours can be knitted up to match different outfits; non knitters can use cuffs off old jumpers.

Elastic topped trousers and a cardigan, instead of a pullover, can be used for men.

Laundry

In the winter, after the worst has dripped off clothes on a drier over the bath, central heating radiators are useful for the carer who does not have a washing machine, spin drier or tumble drier.

Activities

Alzheimer's disease sufferers, rather like children, often need affection, comfort and entertainment.

A firm cuddly toy can be a source of great comfort to the individual. It may become a friend and be talked to as a companion and, at times when the carer is out of favour, remarks in reply to that person may be directed at the toy. The toy also has the advantage that it can often help the patient to relax and, in addition, can be used as a prop for the head when in bed.

It is possible, too, to have a great deal of fun with simple games such as 'The house that Jack built', but it is usually necessary to help. Jigsaws can give great pleasure, even if they are never completed.

Art work can be very entertaining for the sufferer and also provide a form of occupational therapy. Collage is worth trying as pictures can be made by cutting out shapes from coloured paper and sticking these onto paper or cardboard. An effective daffodil can be made from green paper for the leaves and stem, and yellow paper for the outer petals. The trumpet can then be made by using the centre of an egg box, which, when painted yellow, can be stuck to the centre of the flower. Another idea is to use small pieces of coloured tissue paper which, when crumpled up, can be pasted on to cardboard making an attractive picture or design. These and other ideas can be developed to provide an enjoyable pastime. Everything should be kept as simple as possible, for the sake of both the patient and the carer.

It is wise to cover the controls of the television with a small cardboard box that can be easily removed, but which is less likely to attract busy fingers than are shiny knobs.

Telephone

An amplifier in the headset of the telephone, obtainable from British Telecom, allows patients with impaired hearing to continue talking to their friends, thereby retaining social contact, even if they are confused and if what they say does not make sense. It gives sufferers a great deal of pleasure to feel they are communicating. An upstairs telephone extension can be a real bonus and one should, if possible, be fitted. If the extension has a plug, it can be kept in the carer's room but can be plugged in by the patient's bed as required.

Furniture

A small wardrobe and dressing table containing only a few garments will be useful, as the sufferer is likely to start taking everything out continually, and this way there is less to put back. Winter clothing can be kept in another room during the summer, and vice versa.

An armchair with firm arm rests, a high back and 'wings' to support the head is best. A footstool is useful; as well as resting the feet it can be used to delay the sufferer getting out of the chair while the carer goes to the front door or undertakes any other activity that necessitates leaving the sufferer for a few minutes. Finally, a dining room chair with arms is best as it will give more support and help the sufferer to sit down and get up (see page 43).

Holidays

A carer who wants a break and wishes to take the sufferer as well can contact agents who specialise in this area (see pages 39–40).

Tax relief

Whether tax is in the form of rates, community charge (Poll Tax), or anything else, you must enquire as to what rebate you are entitled as soon as you commence caring. Refunds or rebates are generally not made retrospectively. In 1990 severe dementia was made a reason for exemption from Poll Tax.

The Middle Stages

Many of the areas outlined for the early stages of Alzheimer's disease are applicable to the middle and late stages, but additional hints are given here for each of the latter stages. In the middle stages, the carer should try to retain a semblance of normality and continue talking to the patient as if nothing is wrong. Every now and then a sensible reply will be given; this could be by accident or could represent a lucid moment.

If the patient thinks that people who have died (such as parents) are still around the carer should explain that they have 'gone to Heaven' or use a similar expression, employing an idea that has been known from childhood and is easily understood by the patient. This attempt to remain honest and retain reality helps both the patient and the carer.

It is important to keep everything from clothing to cooking and room arrangement to routines as simple as possible, as complicated situations will often confuse the sufferer and make him irritable and frustrated. If carers find themselves getting cross with their patient, they should ask themselves, 'How can I manage this situation better?' Often the answer is to adapt something to be more simple for both patient and helper.

Safety

Sometimes there are shiny metal strips in doorways that keep the edge of the carpet down. These can make patients think that there is a step, so they will step high in a dangerous way. To prevent this, the strips should be painted over in a dark colour.

A baby alarm, kept by the bed, can be a very useful piece of equipment as it will alert the carer to the sufferer's movements during the night. This is especially important if the patient is getting up and needing help in the night, or needs to be stopped from wandering. A good baby alarm (British Standard Approved) can be bought at Mothercare. There are also special plugs that can be placed in ordinary sockets and which relay sound (see page 44).

A small night-light may comfort the sufferer and will help him or her to see the commode so that it can be used more easily. It is also useful to the carer who can see what is happening without disturbing the patient. Little china night-lights can be bought in Woolworths (a red pygmy bulb disturbs sleep less than a clear one) or, alternatively, dimmer switches can be installed.

Eating and drinking

When a knife and fork become too difficult to use, the sufferer will find a spoon easier to handle. It may also become easier to serve high tea rather than tea and supper.

A thermos flask of tea or coffee, made the night before, is a nice 'reviver' for both the carer and the patient first thing in the morning.

General health and hygiene

If, for any reason, the patient has a spell of vomiting, an attractive bowl should be kept clearly visible in each room. This makes it easier for the carer who can grab it quickly to give to the sufferer to use as a vomit bowl. The GP should be notified about the problem so that he or she can discover the cause and prescribe any necessary treatment.

If the sufferer's ankles become oedematous (puffy), the doctor's advice should be sought. A small feather pillow can be placed under the ankles at night, with the heels clear of the sheet. However, when this method is used, the ankles should be massaged regularly. During the day, when the patient is sitting in a chair, a footstool can be used.

Although this seems like a trivial point, it is important to have a soap dish that has sloping sides, like an avocado dish, rather than a conventional flat dish. Alternatively, a soap pad with suction discs could be used, as both will enable the patient to pick up the soap more easily.

Paper towels in the bathroom and kitchen are useful for drying hands, as this saves the carer some washing. These should be put in the dustbin rather than down the lavatory as they can cause a blockage.

Continence problems

If the patient is able to use a commode, there are several ways in which the carer can help. For example, if a few sheets of soft lavatory paper are placed on the edge of the commode, this will alert the patient to the fact that they should be used, especially when he or she is using the commode without help. By doing this, the chances that the patient remains dry will be increased.

If the sufferer tends to wander past the commode while looking for it, a piece of clothes-line around the bed and commode will help. The line can be attached to the end of the bed, passed through the arms of the commode and around the back of it and then tied to the other end of the bed. This will aid the patient as he or she will have to stop to untie the string in order to go beyond the commode.

When the sufferer regularly unties the clothes-line, it will be important for the carer to give assistance in using the commode. At this stage, the baby alarm becomes even more essential.

When incontinence becomes a problem at night, a good rubber sheet is essential. There is an excellent one produced by the Pentonville Rubber

Company (see page 44); this is 3 ft. wide, of medium weight and can be cut to any length required. It is better to use rubber rather than plastic as plastic tears more easily and creates much more condensation. Absorbent sheets are available, but because of their weight after they have been soaked, it is not practical to hand-wash them.

During the day, disposable nappy liners or pads can be worn inside pants to protect the underwear. However, these should not be thrown down the lavatory as they can block the drains.

Double incontinence can present many problems, but there are a number of practical ways by which the carer can minimise the cleaning of both the patient and clothing. After initial washing, a good aid to cleaning the sufferer is eau de cologne (Boots sell an economical one) on cotton wool, but the carer should be careful not to touch delicate parts with the cologne. Drapolene is an excellent cream to use on skin that becomes wet or sore, and the doctor can prescribe this.

Very messy pants can be dropped into the lavatory and left to soak (rubber gloves placed on the edge of the lavatory will remind the carer not to flush it in error). This method ensures that most of the faeces are removed before actual washing begins, especially if the pants are held under the running water several times.

If the patient is suffering from diarrhoea, the GP should be consulted. A good home remedy is arrowroot, which is obtainable from the chemist. Codeine linctus helps too, but this should not be given unless the GP has recommended it. The GP should also be consulted if the individual has constipation; good home remedies for this are bran, prunes and spinach.

Waste disposal

Black dustbin liners are very useful for the disposal of wet incontinence pads and rolls, and in some areas, they are supplied by the community nurse. They can be left out with the dustbin, but it is preferable to organise specialist refuse collection such as that used by stoma patients if this is a service offered locally.

Bedding

Sleep and comfort are important areas of care, and certain measures taken by the carer can promote them. If possible, a south facing bedroom should be used, as this will ensure that the patient has a warm and sunny room. Also, by placing the head of the bed against an inside wall, the patient will be warmer and feel more protected.

A heavily-lined, long pair of curtains is useful at night as they ensure darkness in the bedroom, which may help to persuade the individual that it is night-time and time to sleep. A thinner pair of curtains, behind the first set and on a shorter rail, can help to keep the sun off the individual's eyes when resting or reading in bed during the day.

When the periods of time that the patient spends in bed increase, it is important to ensure comfort. A soft pillow on the top of the triangular pillow will help to stop the head rolling sideways. Another way of using pillows is to place them in the shape of an armchair (i.e. two pillows placed diagonally on top of a base pillow and another placed on top of these).

The right combination of bedclothes for the different seasons is important to ensure that the patient is neither too hot nor too cold.

Clothing

It is better to provide clothing that is easily put on or removed. For example, if the patient is a woman, a dress is more practical than a combination of blouse, jumper, skirt and jacket. If shoulder straps cause discomfort by slipping off, they can be secured by tying them together with a piece of tape. A man's clothing can present more problems, but zips and buttons can be replaced by press-studs.

In winter, a woman's nightdress can be made much easier to handle if it is slit up the front and Velcro fastening attached to both sides. Men's pyjamas can also be fastened with Velcro. In summer, front-buttoning polyester/cotton housecoats are ideal for use as a nightdress. Suitable material for summer and winter clothing should be considered.

A man's large cotton handkerchief, folded and tucked in around the back of the patient's neck, like a scarf, will help to keep out draughts. This can be especially helpful when the patient is in bed, and the handkerchief is easily washed.

The sufferer can be kept warm by wearing long socks over stockings or tights to keep the feet warm, and knitted wristlets or mittens will help to keep the hands warm.

The carer, who has to leap out of bed several times in the night, will find it a good idea to sleep in a woollen pullover in the winter. By doing this, he or she will require fewer bedclothes, and it will save time in reaching the patient while, at the same time, maintain warmth. For the same reasons it helps to wear a pair of pants.

Laundry

In the interests of hygiene, it is important to have one pair of rubber gloves that are used solely for incontinence washing. To differentiate these from any other pair in the house, it is wise to buy them in a different colour. The best types of washing powder to use when incontinence is a problem are those containing biological enzymes, such as Bold and Ariel.

Incontinence can substantially increase the amount of laundry and if the carer does not own a tumble drier, this will necessitate an increase in hanging space for wet clothes. Additional space can be gained by attaching strings over the bath between hooks on the wall, and these can be used for wet pants and other small items.

Activities

In addition to a cuddly toy as mentioned in the previous section, a sand-filled toy, such as a frog, can be excellent, as it can be pulled when the patient is busy groping for things. Other soft toys, with legs and arms that can be held, are also good.

The Alzheimer's disease sufferer may enjoy a number of other children's toys such as picture books, a string of beads to hold (for example children's wooden ones or 'worry beads'), a bubble-blowing set (but the helper will have to help to make the bubbles) and helium-filled balloons tied to the bed-post. These and other toys will usually be appreciated by the patient and will prove to be a source of comfort as well.

When the sufferer finds it difficult to hold a pen and writing becomes a problem, the Disabled Living Foundation, and other similar organisations, can give advice about writing equipment. In general, pens and pencils that need very little pressure and have thick barrels are best. Also, placing a hand on the patient's hand will help to steady it. At first it helps to dictate words, and later spell them out.

A colour television beyond the end of the sufferer's bed will provide a great deal of entertainment. It can become very real to the patient who may object that the carer is rude if he or she speaks when someone on the television is talking.

Later Stages

Throughout their illness, individuals with Alzheimer's disease require a variety of types of stimulation, but this is especially important in the later stages when they are likely to be more passive.

It may become more difficult for the patient to focus on the television, and music can be played as a pleasant alternative. A great deal of pleasure can be given, for instance, by playing records of old well-known tunes, singing favourite songs or playing a musical box.

The variety of soft toys can be increased and specific ones chosen that are made from different materials. In this way, they will not feel alike and the patient's tactile experiences will be increased.

Many different toys can be bought; these could include soft toys made from smooth or furry material, a clown swinging on a bar, a metal man on a cycle swinging between poles, a sand-filled frog and a deflated balloon, which can be screwed up in the fingers making an interesting rustling sound.

Eating and drinking

Eating invariably becomes a problem for the Alzheimer's disease sufferer in the later stages, and it may become necessary to have cold, simply prepared food. The patient can be fed more easily with food such as little pieces of ham, cheese and tongue balanced on each other and popped into the mouth. This was necessary with my mother as she took so long to chew a mouthful and, if left with a plate of food, picked it up by one edge even if it contained gravy. Other nutritious but easily eaten foods can be offered, such as pâté and mousses.

If the sufferer finds it difficult to eat solid foods, there are numerous nutritious drinks or soups that can be given. Complan is invaluable, as are home-made beef tea and marrow-bone soup. Build-Up, which is made in several flavours, is another nourishing drink, and this and Complan can be bought from a chemist. Instant hot chocolate mixes make a pleasant and quickly made drink. In addition, Caloreen can be added to drinks to provide glucose, and Abidec to give vitamins; the GP can prescribe both of these.

When a cup can still be held without assistance but is often spilt, the plastic backed Inco Pads (intended for incontinence use and obtainable through the community nurse) make a splendid 'bib'. If the patient no longer enjoys a cup of tea but wants something warm to drink first thing in the morning, a cup of hot water quenches the thirst, and it does not matter so much if it is spilt everywhere (providing that the hot water does not go over the patient). When help is needed to take a drink, a teaspoon is very efficient and may prove easier to use than an invalid cup.

General health and hygiene

If the patient clamps his or her teeth shut against a toothbrush, the carer can push a finger (with toothpaste on it) around the mouth and teeth quite easily. In this way the teeth can be partially cleaned, which is better than nothing. A piece of disposable J-cloth can be wrapped round the finger for greater hygiene.

Ill people are prone to lip soreness, and Vaseline or Lypsyl, applied frequently to the patient's lips, will help to stop them drying and cracking.

It can be very difficult for the carer to look after the patient's hair, but a comb dipped in water can help to keep the hair clean. A dry shampoo can be useful too, particularly if washing is not tolerated. Tangled hair presents a problem, and can be alleviated by the use of conditioner if it is still possible conveniently to wash the individual's hair. If not, an old fashioned product, oil of violet, can be applied to dry hair and is helpful in removing tangles. If bad dandruff occurs where the head leans on the pillow, eau de cologne or glycerine can be used.

Some beds have removable head-boards, and, in these cases, it is often easier for the carer to wash the patient's hair. The best method is to pull the person up the bed so that his or her head is partially hanging over the head of the bed. The bed should be protected by a waterproof sheet beneath the head, and a bowl should be placed on the floor. The carer can then wash the hair by pouring water over the head from a jug. However, many Alzheimer's sufferers are frightened if their heads are put back in this way.

It is important to prevent muscle wasting, even when the patient is relatively immobile and unable to get out of bed without assistance. One form of physiotherapy is to place a rail on the inside wall of the landing opposite the banisters; with the help of another person, the carer can usually encourage very frail patients who are bedridden to take a few steps while holding onto both rails. We did this every afternoon, with a helper who could assist from behind while I encouraged my mother forward.

Witch hazel applied on cotton wool is excellent for a hot forehead. It can also be used for bruises and sprains, but Witch Doctor is better for these.

Continence problems

As incontinence increases, it is best not to use a sheet on top of the rubber sheeting (see page 44) on the bed. When ordering a length of rubber sheeting, order it a foot longer than actually needed, as if it is too small, it will be easily pushed aside. The large size IPS Pant Liner Pads can be used instead of the ordinary sheet. As they are all tissue, they are comfortable for the patient to lie or sit on, and do not cause condensation as do the plastic-backed ones. They are available from the community nurse or health visitor.

To stop the top sheet becoming wet, place an IPS protective Pant Liner Pad across the top of the patient with a length or square of rubber on top of that.

When the sufferer is in bed, the Velcro of the nightdress should be undone below the waist and the skirt comfortably folded up (not rolled) behind the shoulders. If one of a pair of Kanga pads is placed across the small of the back below the nightdress, it will help to keep the nightdress dry.

The Velcro-side-fastening Kanga pants may be worn both night and day unless the patient becomes very ill. A piece of Inco Roll placed between a pair of Kanga Pads inside the Kanga pants works quite well for a woman.

Although, in the later stages, the commode may no longer be used very often for its intended purpose, it is still worth establishing a regular pattern once a day. Often, the patient will be able to open his bowels although he may not be conscious of doing so. This routine will also give the carer the opportunity to make the bed.

While the patient is sitting on the commode, a warm room is essential. If the patient has a sand-filled frog, it can be put on the immersion heater or radiator for some hours beforehand and used to keep the patient's knees warm; it is slow to lose heat, and is safer than a hot-water bottle. The patient can be kept warm by wrapping an old piece of blanket around the legs, and by putting an IPS Pant Liner Pad across the knees. Tissue handkerchiefs can be placed on the patient's knees to catch dribble.

Comfort is essential, too. If the commode is making marks on the patient's skin, a piece of foam can be cut to fit over the seat and a hole cut in the middle. Foam can also be cut to tie on the arms of the commode to prevent chafing. A big, soft sponge behind each buttock will also help, as will a firm toy placed behind the spine with one or two more soft sponges. (The toy used to help support the head in bed will do splendidly.)

If the patient has reached a very floppy stage, a chair with cushions and pillows on it can be placed to one side so that the patient can rest his or her head and shoulder on it while sitting on the commode.

A length of webbing around the sufferer can be used as a safety harness to prevent falling from the commode or any chair. It is wide enough not to cut into the skin and it can be purchased at a sports shop that caters for climbers. When getting the sufferer off the commode, it is easier if the bed is an old-fashioned one with a bed post at the foot that the patient can hold on to. A sponge placed against the base of the post will stop the patient's toes sliding into it. Similarly, an old mattress on the floor under the bed will stop the sufferer's feet sliding underneath it. A skid could result in the patient catching his or her shin on the edge of the bed, bruising it badly or even breaking the fragile skin in an area that is slow to heal.

Pressure sores

The general care to prevent pressure sores, which was outlined in the previous section, should continue. The carer should also use sponges under the patient's elbows and massage these areas to help in the prevention of sores.

Bedding

A double-bed blanket and sheet that are tucked into the bed on one side and pulled over the sufferer will help to stop draughts on one side. This is particularly useful if he or she pulls at the bedclothes.

Lifting

The community nurse or domiciliary physiotherapist will be able to teach the carer about lifting techniques such as those used to lift a patient who has slipped down the bed.

A good way for carers to get the patient back into bed when they are on their own and the patient can only help a little is to sit on the bed near the pillow, sit the patient on their knee and swing both of them back into the bed. I wore a track suit that had 'give' in it after I found that skirts became trapped under my mother. If the helper is doing anything very active like this, stretch clothes are essential. Stretch trousers and tops can be bought at sports shops, and cotton tee-shirts can be worn with them; all are easily washed.

When helping someone up from a chair ensure their head is forward in line with their feet to make sure their balance is correct.

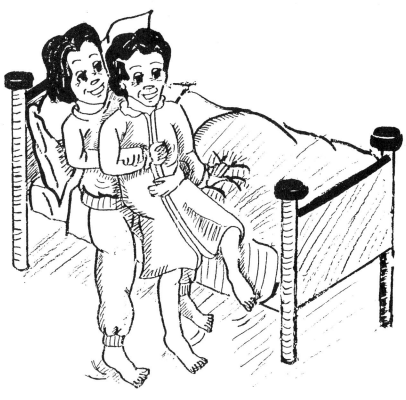

Figure 5

Turntables

Small turntables are now available, which can be used to help move someone (for instance from chair to commode) by putting their feet on it while turning him.

Falls

If the sufferer falls on the floor, it may be necessary to get help. In some areas, it will be possible to contact a neighbour. If not, the ambulance or police may have to be called and they will come as soon as possible. (It is important to check these details before an emergency arises.) While waiting for help, it is important to keep the sufferer as warm and comfortable as possible.

If a mobile person has fallen on the floor, encourage them to roll over face down so they can pull their knees up under them which should make it possible for them to pull themselves up.

The End

If possible, decisions about funeral arrangements should be made well in advance of the sufferer's death, as it is difficult to think clearly and act effectively when the person dies. Sudden decisions can be very difficult, and it is better to make enquiries about funeral directors and related topics when the patient is still alive. People who could be approached for information, apart from friends, include the GP, district nurse and neighbours. The most expensive funeral directors may offer a service that is too elaborate so carers should not be afraid to 'shop around'. It should be decided in advance what type of coffin is required, whether this should be lined or unlined, and whether the sufferer's own clothes or robes provided by the funeral directors are to be used.

Carers might find it useful to have all the essential telephone numbers listed on one piece of paper so that they do not have to hunt for them when the sufferer dies. This list should include the doctor, district nurse, minister of religion and funeral director.

Certifying death

When the sufferer has died, the carer should notify the GP, who will then visit the house to certify death. It is best to take the precaution of asking him to bring a death certificate, as a day's delay may be caused if he does not do so.

Last rites

If the carer and/or patient are religious and want a final blessing from their religious leader, this should be arranged. Sometimes, it is possible to have the blessing before death occurs, but often this is not the case and it then takes place after death.

When the doctor has certified death, the last rites can begin. The only thing that would delay this is if a post mortem is required before a death certificate can be issued or is requested by the next of kin for brain research, this should be arranged long before death.

The carers may wish to help to prepare the deceased for burial or cremation, and if so, they should discuss this in advance, when the details will be explained to them. In most cases the funeral director will make the necessary preparations. If the carer wants the deceased to be washed at home, it is important to check with the funeral directors that they will do this; some do not.

Cremation or burial

The nature of the funeral service should be decided beforehand to prevent any unnecessary problems during the immediate period of mourning. If, for example, the patient wanted to be cremated, this should be recorded beforehand. A good place to do this is in the Will.

Flowers, wreaths and donations

The sufferer's wishes on floral tributes should be respected and the funeral directors notified about the preferred arrangements. If, for example, the patient preferred flower arrangements to wreaths, the carer should specify this, stating the colours for both flowers and ribbons to be used.

If flowers are not wanted, or are only to be accepted from those people present at the funeral, friends and relatives should be informed. The card sent out to tell them about the sufferer's death, or a newspaper announcement, could include a sentence such as, 'If desired, donations to his/her memory may be sent to ...'. A charity in which the patient was interested (or the charity connected with the disease from which the patient suffered) can be named. This allows distant relatives and friends to participate if they so wish.

After the funeral

The British Red Cross Society, occupational therapists and other organisations who have lent equipment, should be informed of the patient's death and arrangements made for the collection and return of the equipment. Items borrowed from the hospital, such as deaf aids or walking frames, should also be returned.

If any tissues, pads or incontinence rolls are on order, these should be cancelled and surplus materials returned. Services such as chiropody will also have to be cancelled.

The pension book and allowance book should be returned to the Department of Social Security and, in the case of financial hardship, enquiries should be made as to whether the Social Fund would pay a lump sum to assist this cost.

The carer should register as unemployed as soon as possible, as, even if there is no entitlement to benefit, Home Responsibilities Protection is available for any complete tax year and will reduce the number of years needed to qualify for retirement pension.

If the carer is single and has been receiving the care allowance, there is an entitlement to Unemployment Benefit, but, as it is quite usual for the authorities to overlook this regulation, it is necessary for the carer to be firm and ask them to look into this further. Married carers should check the current ruling with their local DSS office.

There is a limit to how much one may earn before having Unemployment Benefit stopped, so it is essential to ask about this before taking any casual employment while looking for a full-time job. The rules regarding the actual amount vary from time to time.

Part 3 WHO CAN HELP YOU?

The carer of an individual with Alzheimer's disease can often feel isolated, but there are a number of agencies, organisations and individuals who can be approached for advice.

Caring Organisations and Individuals

Age Concern

The address of Age Concern can be found in the telephone directory. They publish excellent booklets listing local facilities in each area. In some areas, they have day centres, or people who will sit with the patient or do other needed jobs, such as shopping or cleaning windows. They will give advice about the help that is available in your locality, and even if they cannot do something themselves, they normally know who will be able to help.

Alzheimer's Disease Society

This society aims to give help and advice to those who are caring for patients with Alzheimer's disease or related disorders (which includes all those with presenile and senile dementia). They have produced booklets, leaflets and information sheets to help carers. Their address is 158–160 Balham High Road, London SW12 9BN. Tel: 081-675 6550/57/58/59. Other addresses: Northern Ireland Regional Office, 113 University Street, Belfast, BT7 1HP. Tel: 0232 439192. Jersey Branch of the Alzheimer's Disease Society, 10 The Grange, Dongola Road, St Helier, Jersey, Channel Islands. Tel: 0534 39422. Branches will be able to help with local advice and possibly with sitters.

Separate societies: Alzheimer's Scotland, 33 Castle Street, Edinburgh. Tel: 031-225 1453. The Alzheimer Society of Ireland, St. John of God, Stillorgan, Co. Dublin. Tel: 0001-88282. Alzheimer's Carers Association, Camelia, Houmet Lane, Vale, Guernsey, Channel Islands (includes Alderney, Sark, Herm, Jettou and Brechou). Tel: 0481 45652.

Bank manager

Before a patient becomes very confused, the bank manager's advice should be sought about having Authority One so that the carer can deal with the patient's banking, during the later stages of the illness.

Benevolent trusts

Patients or carers who have belonged to the armed forces, police, fire service or some similar organisation may find that the relevant benevolent trust are prepared to help if the carer is subject to a particularly heavy expense for which he or she has only limited funds.
Useful addresses are:

* The Royal United Kingdom Beneficent Association
  6 Avonmore Road, London W14 8RL. Tel: 071-602 6274.

* SSAFA (Soldiers, Sailors and Airmen's Families Association)
  27 Queen's Gate, London SW1H 9B2. Tel: 071-222 9221.

* King George's Fund for Sailors
  1 Chesham Street, London SW1X 8NL. Tel: 071-235 2884.

* The Royal British Legion
  48 Pall Mall, London SW1Y 5JY. Tel: 071-930 8131. Or approach your local branch.

* The Royal Air Forces Association
  43 Grove Park Road, London W4 3RX. Tel: 081-994 8504.

The Carers National Association

This is a new association which has combined the National Council for Carers and their Elderly Dependents (NCCED) and the Association of Carers, and groups are being organised in many areas. It helps those who are caring for anyone, regardless of the reason for the dependence. There is a bi-monthly newsletter. The aims include support for carers, pressing for increased resources, informing relevant bodies of carers' needs and providing a setting for carers to meet without their dependents. In some areas local members will help carers by sitting with a sufferer, or will undertake some similar task. The head office address is 29 Chilworth Mews, London W2 3RG. Tel: 071-724 7776.

Charity Search

This assists elderly people in financial need to find the charities which may be able to help them with, for example, retirement or nursing home fees or if in their own home heating bills, telephone bills or unexpected repair bills for an essential care or in fact any situation which may enhance the viability of staying there.

Charity Search, 25 Portview Road, Avonmouth, Bristol BS11 9LD
Tel: 0272 824060 (10am – 2pm)

Chemists

Most chemists will deliver medicines free to the carer's home if requested.

Chest, Heart and Stroke Association

Dementia can occur after a stroke, and if this is the case, relevant material is obtainable from The Chest, Heart and Stroke Association, Tavistock House North, Tavistock Square, London WC1H 9JE. Tel: 071-387 3012.

Chiropodist

The GP or health visitor can be asked about local clinics and about how the patient's name can be added to their lists. Domiciliary visits are difficult to arrange, but a private chiropodist will usually call, although it is necessary to find one who does not have a full list, which may involve approaching several chiropodists before one will agree.

Churches

Some Churches have schemes to help their members, so it is worth asking them about this.

Citizens' Advice Bureau

The local Citizens' Advice Bureau may be able to help with some problems, and if they are not able to do so, they will be able to refer you to someone who can.

Community Health Council

The Community Health Council office in your area will have leaflets of interest, such as 'Patients' Rights'. They will also be able to give information about facilities in the area, and will do their best to help with any problems that you have encountered during contact with the National Health Service. For instance, they have lists of nursing homes and will know which ones take incontinent patients.

Community psychiatric nurses

These will give a carer a great deal of support and advice as they specialise in dementia and related problems. Your GP will refer you to them or in some cases they may be rung direct.

Council for Voluntary Service (or Council for Voluntary Advice)

Both are listed in the telephone directory under specific counties. These organisations will know of facilities in specific areas, and may have volunteers available to help carers.

Counsel and Care for the Elderly

This organisation keeps a list of good homes in the London area, gives advice to relatives and helps with nursing home fees anywhere in the UK. Their address is 131 Middlesex Street, London E1 7JF. Tel: 071-621 1624.

Counselling services

If a carer feels the need for a counselling service, but is unsure of the facilities available in the area, advice and information can be sought from the doctor, Age Concern or the Citizens' Advice Bureau.

Crossroads Care Attendant Trust

This group will help with physical disability problems, but, in many areas, it does not have the resources to help with psychological or psychiatric difficulties, although more of the groups are now expanding into this area.

CRUSE

CRUSE is an organisation that gives advice and help on bereavement. It has a good social programme and is listed in the local telephone directory. The head office address is 126 Sheen Road, Richmond, Surrey TW9 1UR. Tel: 081-940 4818.

Dentist

Dental care can be given at home. If the visit is made under the National Health Service scheme, the dentist will only make the usual charge for treatment. Check each time with the receptionist that the call will come under the NHS as each visit requires new forms to be signed and these must be brought by the dentist. If the sufferer is having private treatment, the call-out charge should be checked with the receptionist as a private visit can be very expensive.

Department of Social Security (DSS)

Application for the **attendance allowance** should be made for the patient through the DSS, who will supply the appropriate forms. If the helper has given up work to care for the patient, the DSS will give the helper a form to apply for the **care allowance**, after the attendance allowance has been awarded.

The pension book is supplied by the DSS and it is important, before the sufferer becomes too confused, to arrange for someone to call so that they can arrange for the carer to sign for the patient's pension.

Dietician

If the carer wishes to have advice from a dietician, the area health authority will be able to put him in touch with one.

Disabled Living Foundation

The Disabled Living Foundation publishes a useful series of information sheets and booklets, which may be purchased from the headquarters. The subjects covered in these information sheets include beds, chairs, communication, eating and drinking aids, leisure activities, hoists and lifting equipment, sport and physical recreation (facilities for disabled people), personal toilet, personal care, walking aids, transport, wheelchairs, household equipment, household fittings, clothing, clothing fastenings, footwear and incontinence. They can be obtained from Disabled Living Foundation, Information Service for the Disabled, 380–384 Harrow Road, London W9 2HU. Tel: 071-289 6111.

Disablement Information and Advice Line (DIAL)

DIAL aims to advise and help anyone coping with disability. It is a new organisation that is rapidly expanding. If DIAL do not know the answer to a problem they will try to find a solution for the carer, and in some areas they can give practical help, too. Their address is National Association of Disablement Information and Advice Services (DIAL UK), Victoria Buildings, 117 High Street, Clay Cross, Derbyshire S45 9DZ. Tel: 0246 86 4498.

District nurse

In most areas, district nurses will teach carers about basic nursing care. They will also be able to visit the house to give the carer help and to perform some of the more technical tasks.

Doctor

Your GP will arrange visits from the health visitor, the community nursing service, the community psychiatric nurse, the physiotherapist and the occupational therapist when these are needed. If the carers feel that they are not getting the advice or help they need, it may be necessary to change to another GP, and carers should not hesitate to do so.

Emergency services

The ambulance service can be contacted and will help to lift people off the floor if the carer cannot manage. They will also help to make people comfortable and check that they are not hurt. This will be fitted in between emergency calls, so there may be some delay. In some rural areas the police will help if the ambulances have a long way to come.

'Fish' scheme

This was originally organised through Churches to help carers in many neighbourhoods. It is not necessary to be a Church member to benefit. The tasks that can be undertaken vary from one area to another, so the carer should ask the organiser about this.

GRACE

GRACE (Mrs. Gould's Residential Advisory Centre for the Elderly) keep details of private nursing homes outside London. Their address is PO Box 71, Cobham, Surrey KT11 2JR. Tel: 0923 62928. A registration fee is charged.

Health Education Council (HEC)

The HEC is a good source for free leaflets, especially 'Who Cares'.

Health visitor

Health visitors have a separate appointment system from that of their GP, so it is important to make an appointment specifically with the health visitor if advice is needed. Carers have a right to ask the health visitor for advice about most subjects when they need it.

Holidays

- BREAK provides holidays in three holiday centres for elderly people, including those who are confused and incontinent, in order to give carers a break, although carers can stay as well if they wish. BREAK can be contacted at 20 Hooks Hill Road, Sheringham, Norfolk NR26 8NL. Tel: 0263 823170.

- The Combat Care Home is a small home mainly for those with Huntingdon's Chorea, but if room is available they will take Alzheimer's disease sufferers with or without their carers. The Combat Care Home is at Theydon Road, Theydon Bois, Epping, Essex CM16 4DY. Tel: 0378 77588.

- Holiday Care Service gives free advice to carers, tailored to their individual needs, but should be given as much notice as possible. If the carer wants a holiday helper to accompany him, Holiday Care Service will arrange a meeting beforehand to ensure compatibility. The carer pays for the helper's accommodation and travel, but has the advantage of being able to leave the sufferer in safe hands when required. Holiday Care Service is at 2 Old Bank Chambers, Station Road, Horley, Surrey RH6 9HW. Tel: 0293 774535.

Home help

In most areas home helps are supplied by the Home Care Service; Age Concern will know the address of the Area Home Help Organiser. A charge may be made for this facility according to circumstances.

Information centre

If there is a local information centre, it will have lists of appropriate facilities in the area.

MIND

Local associations affiliated to MIND exist to help those with mental illness. As Alzheimer's disease is a physical illness, it is not one of their main interests. Age Concern will know the address of the nearest group.

Neighbourly help groups

Some areas have these, often based in a community centre, and Age Concern will know where they are.

Occupational therapists

These people will assess need, and provide such things as bath-seats, stair rails and raised toilet seats.

Public library

There are usually useful lists of local facilities, charities and organisations in the library. Assistants will help you to find relevant information or books and will show you what they have in their catalogues on any subject you need.

'Red Cross'

This is listed in the telephone directory under 'British Red Cross Society'. The Society will lend the carer medical equipment such as wheelchairs, ripple mattresses, commodes, sheepskins, heel muffs, bed pans, urinals, back rests, bed cradles, rubber rings, plastic sheets, feeding cups and raised toilet seats. The amount or type of equipment that is available varies from district to district, so the carer should ask for details about this. In order to borrow some items of equipment, it is necessary to have a letter from the GP, and the British Red Cross Society will be able to advise the carer about this. They also produce a useful handout sheet, 'Hints for Wheelchair Pushing', and can organise beauty care, foot care, manicures, transport (at a nominal cost), craft work, shopping for those who are housebound, and sitters to enable carers to have a break.

Reminiscence therapy

This is a treatment using memorabilia including old photographs. Carers should be aware that taking anyone back into the past could cause problems for them too. See Part I page 4.

The Retirement and Nursing Home Advisory Service

Advice is given on nursing homes, residential homes and sheltered accommodation. There is a registration fee. Cain and Paton, 4 Ives Close, Aldersey Road, Guildford, Surrey GU1 2ET. Tel: 0483 578160.

Samaritans

The Samaritans are listed in the local telephone directory. They are there 24-hours-a-day if the carer is desperate for an ear to listen to his or her troubles, whatever their nature.

Social Services

Caring for a patient at home can create a number of social and financial problems and a social worker's advice should be sought. The social worker should be able to help both the carer and patient with problems at home and with regard to such things as statutory benefits. Social workers can be contacted through Social Services, who also hold lists of homes that have vacancies.

Solicitor

Before a patient becomes too confused, a Will should be made, if at all possible. A solicitor should be consulted about Enduring Power of Attorney, but as the law stands at the moment, this can no longer be obtained once the patient becomes very confused. Court of Protection may be needed later, but is expensive to obtain.

Specialist medical help

Your GP will be able to arrange, when necessary, for a geriatric or psychogeriatric specialist to make an assessment of the sufferer. If young, the sufferer may be referred to a neurologist. It is particularly important to have an assessment done if the carer is thinking of retiring from work in order to look after the patient, because, if a pension is involved, the diagnosis can make a difference to the amount awarded, as voluntary retirement pensions may be less than compassionate release pensions.

Wireless for the Bedridden

This organisation provides radios and televisions for needy house-bound and aged invalids. Wireless for the Bedridden is at 816 Corbets Tey Road, Upminster, Essex RM14 2AJ. Tel: 04022 50051.

Womens Institutes

They may be able to help by supplying sitters.

Womens Royal Voluntary Society

The WRVS organise 'meals-on-wheels' and 'books-on-wheels', visit the sick and housebound, take trolley shops to homes and run chiropody services.

Equipment and Products

Catalogues of equipment

- Carters (J & A) Ltd, Alfred Street, Westbury, Wiltshire BA13 3DZ. Tel: 0370 822203, produce a large catalogue of medical equipment including lifting aids, bathroom aids, walking aids, wheelchairs, commodes and other toilet aids.

- Homecraft Supplies Ltd produces a mail order catalogue with items to help the disabled. Homecraft Supplies Ltd is at Low Moor Estate, Kirkby-in-Ashfield, Nottinghamshire NG17 7JZ. Tel: 0623 755585.

- Keep Able Mail Order Catalogue is available from Keep Able, Fleming Close, Park Farm, Wellingborough, Northamptonshire NN8 3UF. Tel: 0933 679426.

Do-it-yourself chair

A very reasonably priced, wooden 'Captain's chair', with firm arms, is obtainable from many DIY shops. It is suitable for confused people at meal times, as they have support but cannot wander off as easily as they could from a chair without arms. The chair comes in kit form and it is easy to make as it just needs glue, with possibly a little sandpapering to make it fit, and some varnish to protect the wood.

Locks

Digital locks, for which no keys are needed, are obtainable from locksmiths and hardware stores.

Medical goods

Local suppliers of medical goods are listed in the local 'Yellow Pages' under this heading.

Microfurnace

The microfurnace produces an output temperature at least twice that of a conventional fan heater, and, as the air temperature rises, the microfurnace automatically monitors it and cuts its own energy consumption accordingly. It measures 6 in by 6 in and weighs 6 lbs. It is very safe as the steel casing always remains cool to the touch. No part of the furnace near the grill reaches a temperature above the flash point of paper, so, even if paper is pushed through the fine mesh, it will not catch fire. The microfurnace is expensive and it is possible that the DSS may be able to give a grant or a loan to assist with its purchase.

The microfurnace is available from Microtech Distributors, 16 Branksome Hill Road, Collegetown, Camberley, Surrey GU15 4QG. Tel: 0276 35028.

Pressure mat

A pressure mat with a buzzer which will attract a carer's attention when it is stepped on from a chair or bed can be made to individual specification and be obtained from: A T H Ltd, Unit E, Rocker Trade Centre, Broadgreen, Liverpool L14 3NZ. Tel: 051-259 1255/6. It will need to be installed by an electrician.

Rubber sheeting

The Pentonville Rubber Company Ltd supplies excellent medium-weight rubber sheeting (3 ft wide), which can be cut to any length. It is suitable for use under an incontinent person.

The company also make many foam products required by the patient, cut to specified measurements. These are made from flame-retardant foam and include such things as wedges and cushions for the patient to lean on (with a waterproof cover if required). The firm also supply surgical rings in latex foam. The address is Pentonville Rubber Company Ltd, 50 Pentonville Road, London N1 9HF. Tel: 071-837 0283.

Safety funnels

Safety funnels, for use with hot-water bottles, have a ring that allows air to escape so that the hot water cannot suddenly gush up over the top of the funnel. They are made by Select Plastics Ltd, Unit D1, Treforest Industrial Estate, Pontypridd, Mid Glamorgan CF37 5UT. Tel: 0443 853901.

Safety items

The Nursery Furniture Department of John Lewis, Oxford Street, London W1A 1EX. Tel: 071-629 7711 can supply any of the following items: 'Kiddiproof' refrigerator locks, 'lid-loks', cupboard locks, window locks, socket inserts (to prevent things being pushed into electrical sockets), 'nite lites' (which glow when plugged into a socket), smoke alarms and baby listeners. Also available are cordless nursery alarms that relay sound around the house. Similar items may also be available from branches of Mothercare. Non-slip bath-mats are available from most chemists.

Woollen blanket pieces

These are sold by weight. Please state that you are a carer (refer to this book) and that you require small cellular woollen pieces, and give the sizes required. Available from: Earlys of Witney, Witney Mill, Burford Rd, Witney, Oxfordshire OX8 5EB. Tel: 0993 703131.

INDEX

do-it-yourself chair 43
doctor/GP 17, 24, 25, 28, 32, 37, 39, 41, 42
dressing 6, 12
driving, immobilisation of car 14

early signs 2, 3
eating and drinking 7–8, 17–18, 24, 27–8
emergency services 31, 39
emotional needs 8
enduring power of attorney 42
equipment catalogues 42–3
escorts 5

faith 10
fallibility 7
falls 31
fear 10
fireguards 15–16
fires 15–16
'Fish' scheme 39
food processor/liquidiser 18
funeral arrangements 32–3
furniture 22

general health and hygiene 18–19, 24, 28–9
geriatrician 42
grab-handles/hand rails 14
GRACE 39
grief 10
groping 12, 27
guilt 1, 7

hair care 28
handles 14, 16
Health Education Council 39
health visitor 39
hiding things 3
Hints for Wheelchair Pushing (Red Cross) 41
hobbies 5
holidays 5, 22, 39–40
   Holiday Care Service 40
home help 40
hot-water bottles 21, 29
   safety funnels for 21, 44
humour, sense of 5, 6

Inco pads 28
Inco Roll 29

incontinence *see* continence problems
information centre 40
invalid cup 18, 28, 41
IPS protective pant liner pads 20, 29

Kanga pants 19, 29
keeping up appearances 9
kettles 15
keys 14

labelling/note writing 9
last rites 32
Last Will and Testament 42
   and burial/cremation 32
laughing inappropriately 12
laundry 21, 26
lavatory 16
lifting/transfer techniques 30
   off floor 31
lighting 15
liquidiser/food processor 18
loneliness 9, 10
love 1, 6, 10, 11

male urinals 19
massage 10
mats 15–16
   pressure 43
meals 7, 8, 17, 18, 23–24, 27–28
meals-on-wheels 42
medical equipment 41, 42, 43
memory loss 12, 13
microfurnace 16, 43
microwave oven 18
MIND 40
mourning 10, 32

Neighbourly Help Groups 40
night-light 23, 44

occupational therapists 14, 16–17, 33, 39, 40

patience 7, 13
Pentonville Rubber Company Ltd 24, 44
personal space 8–9
pets 8
physiotherapy 29
pressure sores 17, 20, 30
problems experienced by sufferers 1–2, 6, 7, 9, 10, 12, 13